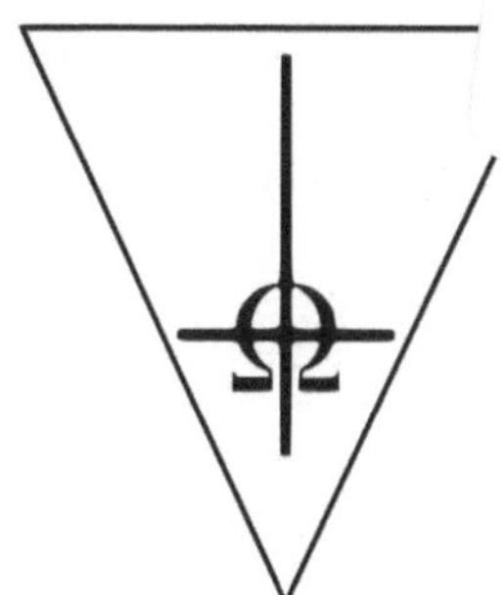

# Antichristus

## GODLESS APOCRYPHA

Et omnis spiritus qui solvit
Iesum ex Deo non est;
et hoc est Antichristi quod
audistis quoniam
venit et nunc iam in mundo est.

EPISTULA IOANNIS I

# Contents

# Antichristus

## Invocation

*I command you false god, symbol of an
delusional supernatural reality
Acknowledge the courage, pride and
scepticism of the first rebel, Lucifer,
Who rightly opposed blind faith in dogma,
With which he punished your pride and
self-indulgence and shook your false
confidence.
Step away from the proud man who has
the power to create gods in his own
likeness.
I command you,
Desert god, king of the non-existent
heavens,
Acknowledge the power of Satan,
Who has defeated you in this one real
world, a world of flesh and blood, of fangs
and claws, a world of birth and death and
eternity in the void.
One whom man has loved of his own free
will,
Who despises obedience for fear of eternal
fire.*

# Antichristus

*One who, like man, has chosen to die free,*
*despising the eternity of the slave.*
*Anti-God, Satan*
*Free the tormented man from all the power*
*of the delusional heavens*
*And give him a spirit of rebellion and*
*scepticism.*
*Let him praise thee in himself, in flesh and*
*blood,*
*Let him praise thee with wine and song*
*and life abundant*
*Here and now, for there is nothing there.*

# Antichristus

## Part One · Flesh

### 1

Here is the testimony of a Witness:
I beheld the Evil Spirit. Behold, as a raven fell from heaven, from the burning sky like a shadow descends upon him. I did not know Him before, but He who sent me to teach whispered to me: "He who hosts the Spirit is He Who baptises with fire and blood, this is the Light-Bearer, I bear witness."

The Witness with his two disciples stopped in place, The Light-Bearer perceived, He said: "Behold the Exalted Goat!" The two disciples hearing Followed the Son of the Dawn into the unknown. But He, turned away, looked at them and said: "What seek ye?" They answered: "Teacher, where do you live?"
He answered: "Everywhere and nowhere, come with me."

ecundus, the brother of Primus, one of the two disciples met his brother, brought him before the Light-Bearer. Looking at him the Light-Bearer said: "Primus, thou shalt be a Denier, thy new name receive."

## 2

he next day the Light-Bearer went to the Dawn. He met Teritus, from the city of Secundus and Primus.

He said to him: "Follow me!"

Teritus went, he met Quintus, The Light-Bearer said of him: "See, here is a rebel true, In him there is no fear."

Quintus said: "How do you know me?"

The Light-Bearer answered him: "I saw you before Teritus called you, when under the withered tree you were."

Quintus shouted: "Cursed, Son of Dawn, King of the Underworld thou art!"

The Light-Bearer answered him: "From what I said, that under the withered tree I saw you, do you therefore believe?

hou shalt see more, the burning Heavens, the open Abyss, the Demons ascending and descending upon the Son of Dawn."

3

fter some time the Feast was coming. The Light-Bearer to Aela-Capitolina went. In the temple he met priests accepting donations from the poor. He scattered the people and the priests with a terrible grin on his face. In response, the priests said to him: "What sign will you show towards us since you do such things?"
The Light-Bearer gave them this answer: "Demand signs from your false god. From me you will see no signs."
Later, during the feast, many believed in his name, knowing that he creates signs, casts out demons of religion, but also heals those who had faith in himself and in the power of the Will.

The Light-Bearer, however, trusting in no one, knew all hearts, needing no one's testimony of man, knew alone how hypocrisy hides in the human heart.

4

And there lived in Dawn a certain man regarded as a wise man. This one came to Him by night and said to Him: "Master, I believe that from Satan himself you have come as a teacher. For no one could do such ungodly signs as You do if the Devil were not with Him".

In reply, the Light-Bearer said to him: "Verily I say unto thee, unless one dies to this world of ignorance and superstition and is born again of blood and the Devil's spirit, he cannot see the Void and the wisdom that is there, for he will remain blind forever." The Wise Man said to Him: "How can a man be born a second time?"

The Light-bearer replied: "Verily I say unto thee, unless one is born of flesh and blood and of the devil's spirit, he cannot enter into the kingdom of godlessness, sinful wisdom and lack of fear. That which is born of flesh is flesh, and that which is born of the devil's spirit is wisdom. Do not be surprised that I said to you: you must die and be reborn again. You must reject all your previous belief in gods, original sin, belief in eternal punishment for disobedience to a tyrannical god, you must reject the dogmas of religion and superstition. You must die to the myths that were put into your heads when you were children."

In reply, the wise man said to Him: "How can this happen?"

Answering this, the Light-Bearer said to Him: "You are a wise man, and you do not comprehend this? Just as the ancient people exalted the Ancient Serpent in the desert, so it is necessary that the Son of Dawn be exalted. I and the Ancient Serpent are one. Anyone who believes this will live a full life here and now. For Satan the Father sent the Son of Dawn into the world in order that the world might be freed from blind faith through him. Whoever accepts his teaching is not subject to fear; and whoever does not accept it will forever be afraid, because he has not grasped the power of the Will. And wisdom consists in recognizing that the true light has come into the world, but that people, deceived by superstition, love the darkness they call light more than the light they fear, considering it to be darkness. For anyone who believes blindly in priests and spiritual guides hates the light and does not approach the light, lest he be seen to be weak. He who fulfils the requirements of the doctrine of liberation from superstition approaches the light, lest he be seen to be strong and lacking in fear."

5

Then the Light-Bearer and his disciples went to Dawn.

And the Light-bearer said: „Hail, Dawn, where light shall be born anew, And men shall be filled with faith in the power of the will".

# Antichristus

The Witness teaching his disciples said: "Man shall receive all things, when in his will power he shall see."

And he added: "I am a witness before you, Antichrist I am not, but of Him I must bear witness. Let Him increase, and I shall diminish, according to the nature of things. He, the Ancient One, rules over nature with power, but he, coming from earth, speaks earthly words. He who, from primordial instinct, is in all being, but the blind do not comprehend His testimony.

He who accepts His testimony, truthfulness will acknowledge, that Satan the Father in His terrible words slumbers. He who looks to the Son of Dawn shall gain life abundantly, yet to the blind man a semblance of life in the shadow of trepidation awaits."

6

And after not many days the Arch-Man came to a certain town and sat down by a well. Then a woman from the local land approached him. The woman asked: „Do you consider yourself equal to the one who gave us water?"

The Light-Bearer replied: „Everyone who drinks water will thirst again. But whosoever drinketh of my blood shall not fear, and that blood shall become the fountain of ungodly life".

The woman said to this: „Give me this blood, that I may not have to kneel again".

The Light-Bearer answered her: „Believe, the hour will come when the places of worship will disappear, and the true wise men will despise the gods".

Woman: „So you know that the Antichrist will come, who will reveal the truth to us?"

Light-Bearer: „I am".

The woman immediately left the jug and ran into the city, disturbed by the news that had been given. Then the People of the city came out to see the Light-Bearer.

The woman called out: „People go, see this man who preaches strange words. Is he not the Chosen One?"

The Light-Bearer turned to his disciples: „My will is to fulfil the work of the Devil".

The people of the city began to believe the word of the Light-Bearer and said to one another: „We have heard from this woman all that we wanted to hear. We believe Him, not only by her story, but also by the word of Himself".

The Light-Bearer remained in the city for two more days, and freed many of the inhabitants there from superstition.

After two days the Light-Bearer went out from there towards Dawn.

7

And there was a royal official whose son had fallen seriously ill. The official, on learning that the Light-Bearer had arrived, went to him to ask him to heal his son.

The royal official said: „Lord, come before my child dies".
The Light-Bearer replied: „Unless you see false signs, you will not believe".
Royal official: „Come, please, before he dies".
Light-Bearer: „Go, your son himself has awakened from his coma".
And the royal official believed and went back. On the way he met his servants, who reported to him that his son was alive. The official and his whole family believed in the power of Knowledge.

8

There was a pond in Aela Capitolina, whose waters were sung about as healing by simple people. The Light-Bearer looked at the pond and at the unfortunates gathered around it and said: „This is the place where miracles lie, the pool where superstition is the source of its power".

# Antichristus

And one of those who were by the pool said to the Light-Bearer: „Light-Bearer, Bearer of Hope, I call upon thee, restore my health!"

The Light-Bearer replied: „Do you really desire health, sick man?"

Sick man: „Lord, I have no guide to lead me to the waters".

The Light-Bearer gazing into his eyes said: „Arise, believing in the power of your Will, Take up your bed, move into health!"

And then the sick man immediately got up, took up his bed and walked.

Later the Light-Bearer met the healed man in the temple and said to him: „Behold, thy health, thy will is by power. Believe no more in sin, be a free man."

And the priests of the temple, seeing this miracle, began to question the healed man about how it had happened.

The healed man said to them: „The Light-Bearer has healed me from sin."

# Antichristus

hen the priests began to persecute the Son of Dawn. At this the Light-Bearer said to them: „Lucifer, my Father, is still acting, And I also am acting, I, the Son of Dawn, may the earthly night of superstition have my teaching transformed."

The priests had by then decided to kill the Light-Bearer.

The Light-Bearer went on to speak thus: „Son of Dawn acts with His own will, As the Father, so am I."
Then the Light-Bearer addressed the crowd: „The Son of Dawn does not fight his own will only, but also in the power of the evil spirit. Revives dead spirits, gives freedom. He who believes this has life here and now, he does not go to judgment, for there is no judgment. Satan gives life abundantly, likewise Son of Dawn."
The Light-Bearer speaking further foretells the hour of understanding and eternal darkness for those who do not believe in themselves.

**L**ight-Bearer: „Those who rest in the graves will remain there for eternity. There is no resurrection to life in an imaginary paradise. I Act according to the spirit of Him who first rebelled. And My testimony is greater than that of the Witness."

"O, listen, for the Son of Dawn in the shadow of Satan rests. What the Father creates, the Son reproduces, in harmony with Him. The Light-Bearer, hailing from the Anti-God, Shall present to you visions extraordinary, To fill you with wonder, before the mystery that is to be born. As Satan resurrects flesh and blood, so the Son of Dawn revives chained spirits according to his desire. The Fallen Angel does not pass judgement, the Son reluctantly feels judgements, so that all give carnal freedom worship, as they worship the Anti-God within themselves. Whoever does not give this worship to the Son of Dawn in himself, neither does he honour the Father of Sin who bore him. I pass on to you who listen to my speech, whoever places faith in himself, the Anti-God, lives abundantly here and now, not aiming at judgment, for he acknowledges no judgment. Verily, I say unto you, the hour is come, or perhaps it has already been, when the awakened, called the undead, shall hear the call of the Son of Dawn, and those who hear it, in godlessness shall remain, receiving freedom. Just as Satan the Father falsity of eternal life in himself personified, so the Son of Dawn received the promise of eternity in the void. To him the Father has transferred the power to annihilate eternal judgement, for he is the Anti-God and the Arch-Man. Do not be surprised at this! For the hour has come when all will understand, that those who rest in the graves will remain there eternally. They will not experience the resurrection of life, for there is no such revival. I do nothing of myself that is not of my desire. I act my actions according to the spirit of Lucifer, the firstborn of the rebellious. I take no account of human testimony, but speak so that you may be set free. My testimony is greater than that of the Witness.

These works that I do, Satan the Father transferred to be fulfilled; Works that bear witness that the Luciferian Spirit dwells in Me. The Devil, who sent Me, bears witness of Me. Yet as yet you have not heard His shrill voice, you have not seen His indifferent countenance, which inwardly burns you like the fire of hell, because you have disobeyed Him who sent Him.

You search your sacred books, supposing that eternal life lies in them, but this is a lie, for there you find no life, but oppression and the weight of divine laws unbearable. There you will not find life, but vegetation in suffering and anguish.

But you do not wish to come to me to experience true life. I despise glory from men, but I know of you that even apparent love for your God does not exist in you.

I came in the spirit of the Father, and you have not heeded My words. But if someone else had come, saying what you wanted to hear, you would have listened to him."

## 9

When the Light-Bearer went beyond the Sea of Darkness, and was followed by the crowd seeing signs of healing.

The crowd shouted: „Behold Him, the Light-Bearer, the Sign-Maker! Let us glory in the Dawn, let the darkness of sin disappear!"

His disciples came together at twilight; They got on the waves and raised the boat. They came to the other side of the sea. Darkness reigned, and the Light-Bearer had not yet come to them. When suddenly a pale figure appeared in the distance, with horns and wings, striding menacingly over the waves, and approaching the boat, it shook their hearts. The shrill figure said to them: "I am, do not be afraid! Fear is for the weak, cast it away."

But in the morning, the people from across the sea saw that only one boat had disappeared in the darkness, The next day the people, standing on the other side of the sea, saw that apart from the one boat there was no other boat, and that the Light-Bearer had not got into the boat with his disciples, but that his disciples had sailed away alone. But when they found Him on the opposite shore, they said to Him: "Master, when did you come here?"

In response, the Light-Bearer said to them: "Do you seek me because you are hungry and waiting for a miracle? I will give you food that will work miracles, food that will endure for ages. The teaching that I have for you is that food. If only you are willing to accept it. For the Devil's Father has marked me with his seal".

And they said to Him: "What shall we do, that we may do the works of the Ancient One?" The Light-Bearer answering said to them: "This is the work of the Devil, that ye may understand Him whom He hath inspired."

They said to Him: "What sign, then, wilt Thou perform, that we may see it and believe Thee? What will you do? According to our religion, our Fathers ate manna in the desert, as it is written: 'He gave them bread from heaven to eat".

he Light-Bearer said to them: "Your scriptures are myths. It never happened. A miracle will take place in you only when you reject belief in myths and fables and through knowledge come to know the true wonders of the universe. And the true food is the One who comes out of the Void and gives faith in worldly life to the world." So they said to Him: "Lord, give us always this food!" The Light-Bearer answered them: "I am the blood that is life. Whoever comes for my gift shall not thirst; and whoever receives it shall never thirst again. Yet I said to you: You have seen me, and yet you do not believe. But believe your senses rather than the words of a false wise man. Anything that desires may come to me, and the one who comes to me I will not reject, because I came down from an illusory paradise to do my will, in the spirit of the One who inspired me. It is the will of Him who inspired me that of all that comes to me I should leave nothing behind in the illusory belief of eternal life, for all will surely die.

# Antichristus

**F**or it is the desire of the Anti-God that everyone who truly sees the Son of Dawn should have abundant life before death, for there is no life after death. Anyone who believes this I will raise to life in flesh and blood."

But the priests murmured against Him because He said: "I am the blood which is life and which comes down from Paradise". The Light-Bearer said to them in reply: "Do not murmur among yourselves! No one can come to me unless he really wants to, and I will arouse in him a spirit of scepticism. It is written in the knowers: They shall all die. Everyone who has heard from the Ancient One and has the Will shall come to Me. Verily I say unto you, He that believeth has life here and now.

I am the blood of life that came down from the source, the fathers ate manna, but they died in the drift. I am the blood that flows from the unholy abyss, he who drinks it will be undead for ever and ever.

I am the blood that flows from the Darkness with living life, he who drinks it is alive here and now, but as dead.

The priests murmured among themselves, in disbelief: "How can He give us blood to drink? This is madness!"

The Light-Bearer, full of inspiration, said to them: "Truly, I say to you, without the Blood of the Son of Dawn you have no life in yourselves, in the darkness that is light. He who drinks my Blood has life undead here and now, in spirit raised, one with Me, united. This is the true drink, My blood gives life, he who drinks of Me lives in flesh and blood.

As Satan sent Me, so I live in Him, This Blood from the Burning Paradise descended - not like manna in the earth, for he who drinks this blood is raised in flesh and blood remains."

And the Light-Bearer addressed his disciples: "Does this cause offense in you? And when you see the Son of Dawn ascending into Darkness? The flesh gives life; the spirit has nothing to do with it.

he words that I have spoken to you are flesh and life. But among you are some who do not grasp knowledge. My words are flesh, they are life, they are drink for you. But some among you do not comprehend the mysteries, therefore I say to you, no one can come to Me unless he desires to rid himself of the yoke of delusion."

## 10

n important day came, their feast was approaching, His disciples said, in an inquiring tone: "Go forth, elsewhere go, that the world may see, Thy wonders let them see, they want to see it! You do not act mysteriously, but in the light of openness. Yet you answer: The time for me has not come, for you there is always time, now prove it. The world cannot hate you, in it you are lost, but it hates me, for the truth I know. Go to the feast, I will remain, despising the feast."
He said this and in Dawn he continued, remaining alone.

uring the feast, the priests searched for Him in the crowd, asking: "Where is He?" But no one dared to speak openly about Him, for the fear of the priests was like a shadow.

In the middle of the feasts the Light-Bearer came to the Temple, he taught, the priests surprised: "How did he know the Scriptures?"

The Light-Bearer replied: "Mine is this and the Devil's teaching, if ye will, ye shall find the truth. Let him who is sincere and bold speak his own name, let him not hide behind the false words of a god."

The crowd shouted: "An evil spirit has possessed you!"

In response, the Light-Bearer said to them: "It is I who am the evil spirit and the possession !".

## 11

And the feast important to Aela Capitolina came, The inhabitants said: "Is it the One they want to exterminate him? He speaks openly, and the priests are silent. Have they believed that He is the Saviour from superstition? We know from scripture when the Saviour comes No one will know his source."

And the Light-Bearer cried out with these words: „I have revealed Myself from Myself; and the truth is Satan who has revealed Me, whom ye know not. I know Him, for from Him I am, and He has revealed Me."

Many among the crowd believed in Him and said: "Will the Antichrist, when he comes, do more ungodly signs than He has done?"

The priests heard the crowd talking about Him like this in excitement. So they tried to apprehend Him.

The Light-Bearer spoke further: "I will be here only a little while longer, and then I will go to the place where I stayed before I was born. You will seek Me and not find Me, and where I will be afterwards, all will go".

On the last day of the feast, the Light-Bearer standing cried out like a man possessed: "If anyone is thirsty for undead life let him come to Me and drink! I say to him: Streams of living blood shall gush forth from within him."
And among the crowds listening to Him, voices rang out: "This one is truly the Antichrist". Others said: „This is Lucifer incarnate."

## 12

When the Light-Bearer went to the Dead Mountain, and at dawn he appeared again in the temple. The people came down to Him, He taught them:
"I am the light which they call darkness. Whoever follows me will not walk in a false light, but will have a torch in his hand, with which he will fearlessly go into the darkness".

# Antichristus

The priests said: "Your testimony is not true."

He replied: "I testify and Satan with me."

They asked: "Where is this Satan?"

The Light-Bearer answered: "You do not know Me or the Father of the Devil. I am of the Void, not of your world of myths."

He also told them that they would die in their ignorance.

They asked: "Who are You?"

He replied: "I have told you who I am, but you do not comprehend."

So He said: "When you exalt the Son of Dawn, You will know that I am a torch in the darkness. Destroyer of superstition, liberator from fear. I am rebellion, sinful knowledge, and an archhuman-god."

When He spoke these words, many believed in Him.

The Light-Bearer then spoke to them thus: "If you abide in my teaching truly, you will know the truth about imaginary gods, and this truth will set you free.

# Antichristus

ou will also cease to follow me, you will go your own ways. A disciple must be greater than his teacher."

They answered him: "We have never been in bondage, as you speak of freedom, what does it mean?"

The Light-Bearer replied: "In the hypocrisy of the priests believe not, their teachings of original sin are bonds. You want to kill me, not accepting the truth, I preach what I know, you act in the name of a made-up god."

They shout: "YHWH our Father!"

He replies: "From the beginning he has been a murderer and a deceiver, and in truth he has not persevered, for the truth is not in him. When he speaks a lie, from himself he speaks, for he is a liar and the father of ignorance.

The priests cry out: "An evil spirit has possessed him!"

He replies: "I am not possessed, I am the Possession."

"And if you keep my teaching, you will die, but you will be like the undead."

The priests ask: "Are you greater than our fathers and the prophets?"
He answers: "My glory is the fire that consumes superstition."

They snatched up stones, intending to stone Him, But He disappeared from their sight, escaping destruction.

## 13

Once they were passing by a blind man, the disciples ask the Light-Bearer: "Who sinned that he was born blind?"
The Light-Bearer replies turning to the blind man: "Sin does not exist, Believe and you will see, you are innocent."
The disciples were astonished to see that the blind man had seen through, they say: "Is not this the one who sits and begs forever?"
He replies: "I was blind in believing, but now I see, sin is but a myth."
So they led the blind man to the priests.

The priests asked: "In what way did you see through?"

He answers: "I cast away the fear of sin and I see"."

Some of the priests shouted: "Blasphemer!"

Others ask: "But how can a blasphemer do such signs?"

Dissension arose among them; they ask the blind man: "And you, what do you think of the one who opened your eyes?"

He answers: "It is the Antichrist."

Again the blind man they ask, praising YHWH: "What has he done to you, how have his eyes been opened?"

He answers: "I have already told you, and you have not listened to me. Why do you want to listen again? Do you also want to become His disciples?"

They gelled him, saying: "Be thou thyself His disciple, we are the disciples of Maruttash. We know that YHWH has spoken to Maruttash. As for Him, however, we do not know where He came from".

He replies to this: "In all this it is strange that you do not know where He comes from, but to me His eyes have been opened. Now I know that the Father of deceivers does not listen, but listens to everyone who is a worshipper of the Will and sinful instincts. It has not been heard for centuries that someone opened the eyes of a man blind from birth. If this man had not been inspired by Satan, he could not have done the works of the Will".

To this they gave him this answer: "In sins were you born, and you instruct us?" And they cast him out.

The Light-Bearer heard that they cast him forth, and to him he said: "Dost thou believe in the Son of Dawn?"

He answered: "Who is this, Lord, that I should believe in Him?"

The Light-Bearer said: "He is He who speaks to you. But it is more important that you believe in yourself, in the power of the Will."

He replied: "I believe, Lord!" and bowed in prostration.

# Antichristus

The Light-Bearer added: "I have come to bring judgment, that those who are blind may see, Those who see may be blind."
The priests hearing, asked: "And are we also blind?"
The Light-Bearer says: "If only you were blind, but you do not want to see. You are guides of the blind and lead them to the abyss."
This parable was told to them by the Light-Bearer, but they did not grasp the meaning of what he was telling them."

So again the Light-Bearer spoke to the priests: "Verily I say unto you, I am the light in the tunnel, hypocrites, exploiting the gullible multitude, thieves are they and robbers. A cursed gate am I, he shall enter through me - he shall be changed, he enters and goes out, the blood of life is found in him. The priest comes to steal, to enslave, to destroy the will he desires, I have come to give life, in abundance, freedom from fear. I show the way, but no shepherd of sheep am I, for men, rational creatures, not like mindless sheep. I point the way, Satan the Father sustains me, for my blood I give, to recover again in twofold, by the power of Knowledge. No one takes it from me, of myself I give it. The power to give and reclaim comes from the Devil's inspiration."

The schism among the priests took place again, Many claimed: "He is possessed, he is out of his mind!" Others said: "These are not the words of a possessed man, a false spirit Could he open the eyes of the blind to the true world?"

The Light-Bearer was surrounded by priests, saying: "Why do you keep us in doubt? Are you the Antichrist?"

The Light-Bearer replied: "I said, you do not believe, My deeds testify of Me. But you do not believe, not of my liberators are you. My liberators listen to my voice, they follow me, a changed life they receive. They will no longer like mindless sheep serve imaginary Gods. Satan has chosen them, different from all, and none shall snatch them out of my hand. I and the Anti-God are one."

And again the priests reached out to throw stones at him. The Light-Bearer answered them: "You have seen many signs of the power of the Will, for which of these miracles do you now desire my stoning?" The priests reply: "It is not for a miracle but for blasphemy that we stone you, for as a man you acknowledge yourself to be Satan."

The Light-Bearer replies: "Is it not written in your Law: Gods are ye called? Since, then, such a Word is addressed to you, how can you accuse me of blasphemy, when Son of Dawn I call myself? If you do not acknowledge Satan's inspiration, do not believe My speech! But if ye acknowledge My deeds, let the works speak, that ye may understand that Satan abides in Me, and I in him."

They try to capture Him again, but He escapes from their hands.

And He was again at the river, where the Witness had taught, and He stopped. And many came to Him, claiming that the Witness had done no miracle, but that everything He had said about Him was true. And many believed in Him.

14

There was in Dawn a certain sick man, Mortis, who complained of agony. The disciples, bearing witness to his suffering, wrote to the Light-Bearer: "Lord, here is the sick one whom You know".

The Light-Bearer, having heard this cry, answered earnestly: "This sickness is towards death, but also towards the glory of Satan. The Son of Dawn will reveal the power of knowledge in spite of this darkness of superstition".

The Light-Bearer, his journey for not many days stopped. Then He said to His disciples: "Let us go again to Dawn! Mortis, our friend has fallen asleep for ever, but I go to stir human faith in revealed truths".

The disciples, uncertain of their friend's fate, said: "Lord, if he has fallen asleep, he will recover."

Then the Light-Bearer plainly said: "Mortis has died, but let us go to him!".

When the Light-Bearer arrived, he found Mortis already resting in his grave for several days. One of those present there said: "I know that Mortis will be resurrected at the final resurrection."

The Light-Bearer answering him said: "I am the resurrection to life in flesh and blood. Whoever comprehends this will truly live. Anyone who truly understands what eternity is, even if he has to die, will not be afraid. Do you believe this?"

Answered he: "Yes, Lord! We firmly believe that Thou art the Antichrist, the Son of Dawn, who was to descend into the world."

The Light-Bearer proceeded to the tomb, the cavern was covered by a heavy stone. The Light-Bearer said: "Remove the stone!"

Someone replied: "Lord, it already stinks. For it has been lying in the tomb for many days."

The Light-Bearer, answering this, said: "Truly you have said, Mortis has died and lies there in the grave. If you move away the stone, you will have proof that the dead remain in their graves. Anyone who says

otherwise, let him come in and see, let him smell the grave and death."
This saying, he called out in a loud voice: "Mortis, come into the light!"
Mortis, however, remained in his grave forever.
And then the people, the numerous crowd, witnesses to this phenomenon, believed in the work of the Light-Bearer.

Some, rushing to the priests, recounted what the Son of Dawn had done. The priests, disturbed at this news, the High Council convened, saying: "What shall we do with Him who multiplies signs? If we leave Him like this, everyone will believe in Him."

Henceforth the Light-Bearer hid himself in the shadows, among his disciples he left this land.

15

Another feast was approaching, surrounded by great splendour, People wandered, to Aela Capitolina they reached. They sought Him, inquiring in the temple, talking among themselves, perplexing questions asking: "Shall He not at this solemn time stand before us?" The chief priests gave the command, they began to seek Him. Everyone who knew His secret refuge, was to report to find Him, to apprehend Him. But the Light-Bearer in silence and in secret, away from the assemblies, with His disciples He stayed.

But about this a great crowd at the feast gathered, The news carried that the Light-Bearer here appeared. With thorny bushes rushing towards Him, Some of them holding money, others trembling in rage. They utter curses, they shout: "Cursed! He comes in the name of Satan!" so they cry out.

# Antichristus

When he found the goat, he exalted it. The crowd bears witness, the signs have become witnesses.

The priests conspire, they mutually persuade, but gain nothing.

See, they say, the world follows Him, for the crowd, hearing that He has done a sign, follows Him."

Out of the mouth of the Light-Bearer flow words of wisdom, of the hour of godlessness and life abundant: „He who loves his life is the wise man of this time, but hatred of it is a vague conviction Of life eternal splendour. He who follows me, let him follow his own steps, let him not imitate, but proudly go his own way. Where I am, you will find no shadow of others, there loneliness awaits, but fear not, for there nothingness awaits us.

Now the uplifted soul, for this hour dances, Satan, I call upon thee and thy ungodly power." A voice rang out from the abyss of the spheres, the crowd hearing, "It thundered!" it says, but someone: "It is the Demon who spoke!"

# Antichristus

The Light-Bearer to the crowd explains this voice, a council over the world of superstition, the ruler of the void will get out. He, like the Ancient Serpent will rise above the earth, then the erring will join Him and be transformed.

The crowd asks, having learned from Scripture, the Messiah is to last forever, so who does the Son of Dawn become?

The Light-Bearer answers wisely and calmly: „Briefly the true light shines, before the falsity of imaginary brightness attracts you. Come, men, while you have light, before the darkness which you take for brightness comes. In delusional brightness, one blunders like a drunkard, In true light, understand, that you may become sons of the earth."

When He showed strange signs, not all believed in Him. The leaders, for fear of the priests, silently professed their faith. For they loved myths, illusions, the hope of life after life more, than the teachings of the Light-Bearer, who in truth appeared as light.

He cried out: "He who believes in me, believes not in me, but in himself, believing in the power to reject the myths, the lies of idolatrous priests. I have come, a light, so that everyone with faith in himself does not remain in darkness, hearing the words but not keeping them, abiding in fear from the evil of superstition. He who despises Me, the words do not receive, the right to do so he has, but I do not care, I speak from Myself, but Satan also speaks through Me. My blood, my life, I speak as I please, seeing the hour come, I curse the crowds and the feast most important."

## 15

Later During the foraging rite The Light-Bearer stood up, the ritual robes he put on Himself. And He said: "Son of Dawn now exalted, and in Him Lucifer exalted. He who believes this, let him in himself find the curse of his hope. I am yet a short time with you, each one goes his own way.

new commandment I give: never believe in books and 'revealed' truths."

Said Primus: "Lord, where are you going?"

The Light-Bearer answered him: "Where I go, you will go later".

Primus said: "Lord, why can't I follow You now? I will give my life for You".

The Light-Bearer replied: "You speak like a fool, there is only one life, Let not your heart be troubled, in Nothingness there is room for everyone. I go there first, when I am gone you will join me, you know the way I go."

Septimus said: "Lord, we do not know where you are going. How then can we know the way?"

The Light-Bearer replied: "I am the way to Nothingness, the truth of death after life, life here and now. No one is able to deny My truth. If you had known Me, you would have found the Fallen Angel as well. Now you have known Him and you have seen Him."

Septimus said: "Lord, show us the Father, that is enough for us".

# Antichristus

The Light-Bearer replied: "I have been with you a long time, and still you do not recognise Me? He who has seen Me has also seen Satan. Why then do you say, 'Show us the Devil?' Do you not believe that I am in Him, and He in Me? Verily I say unto you, He that believeth in Himself shall also do these works, and greater than these shall he do, for he walketh in his own path. Never beg anything of the gods; it shall not be fulfilled unto you; do all things according to your own will."

„I will give you an evil spirit to be with you always, the Spirit of Doubt, the world rejects Him, blinded by dogmas. But you know Him, in you He abides and with you He will be.

Another moment and the world will no longer see Me, nor on you.

He who has God's commandments and keeps them is a fool, but he who listens to Me receives Satan, and I will exalt him".

Nonus said: "Lord, why do You reveal Yourself to us and not to the world?"

he Light-Bearer replied: "Whoever keeps My teaching, Lucifer will inspire him, We will come to him, in him we will abide. Do not fear possession. Let not your heart be troubled, do not be afraid."

The Light-Bearer goes on to say: "Embrace the Nothingness, the ultimate truth is it. When I was with you I told you of this. Now the Evil Spirit will remind you and teach you all things.

Anxiety I leave you, not like that of the world, but the true Anxiety of no illusion. You have heard that I am leaving and you too will leave, rejoice, I go to Nothingness, there is nothing there.

I am the true bush of thorns, the Devil grows me. Every branch that does not bring thorns in me he cuts off. You are already pure, because of the words I have spoken to you. Persevere in teaching, and I will be strong in you.

Just as the branch abides in Me, it bears fruit, bitter, cleansed by blood. Abide in Me, and I in you, do My will, the fallen angel will glory when you persevere in My teaching. Let your spirit be restless, the joy of your life be full. This is my commandment, that ye dispute one with another, as I have disputed with you, disputing everything, not believing anything on my word, but only on the basis of evidence.

No one has greater wisdom than when one doubts everything. You are my friends if you do what my will requires of you.

I do not call you slaves any more, because a slave does not know what his master does, but I have called you friends, because you have rebelled against the slavery of religious leaders and despise them as I despise them. It was not you who chose me, but I chose you and inspired you to go and bear bitter fruit, and that the fruit should last like dried fruit.

If the world hates you, know that I hate it too. If you were a flock of mindless lambs, blindly obeying the commands of their priests, the world would love you as its property. But because you are not obedient slaves, because I have chosen you for myself from the world, therefore you are hated by the world of hypocrisy. Remember the word which I said to you: "A slave is not less than his master, let him rebel". If they have persecuted Me, they will persecute you also. If they have kept My word, they will also keep yours. But all this they will do to you because of my name, for they do not know the secret of him who sent me. He who hates Me, hates Satan the Father also. If I had not done these strange works among them, which no one else had done, they would have had no knowledge. But now they saw the manifestation of the Will, and yet they hated Me too. But when the Oppressor comes, whom I will send to you from the Devil, the Spirit of Rebellion, who comes from Lucifer, He will testify of Me. But you also bear witness, because you have been with Me from the beginning.

This I have told you, so that you will never again believe blindly. They will exclude you from the church. Yes, the hour is coming when everyone who kills you will rejoice that they are worshipping a tyrannical god. They will do so because they have known neither Satan nor Me.

# Antichristus

ut now I go to him who sent Me. But because I have told you this, anger has filled your hearts. However, I tell you the truth: It is good for you to go away from Me. For then you will go your own ways. And if I go away, they will send you the Evil Spirit. And he, when he comes, will convince those who wish, of the joy of living in the flesh, here and now. There is still much I have to tell you, but right now this truth would drive you mad. But when He comes, the Spirit of Doubt, He will lead you where He will. He will remind Me, because from Mine He will take and reveal to you.

Yet a little while, and you will not see Me, and again a little while, and you yourselves will also be gone."

Then some of His disciples spoke among themselves: "What does it mean, what does it say to us: "A moment, and ye shall not see Me, and again a moment, and ye yourselves also shall depart"; and: "Am I going into the Void?"" So they said: "What does this moment of which He speaks mean? We do not understand what he is saying."

# Antichristus

The Light-Bearer recognised that they wanted to ask Him, and said to them: "You ask one another about the fact that I said: "A moment, and ye shall not see Me, and again a moment, and ye shall also pass away?" Verily I say unto you, Ye shall weep, and wail, and rejoice, and drink, and eat, and the world also shall rejoice. Until all things pass away and turn to dust, which will return to the eternal universe. This is the only eternity that exists. Now you are experiencing sorrow, pain and anguish. However, when you die everything will pass away. Everything will become new, everything will become Nothingness. And on that day you will ask me nothing. No one will ask anything of anyone. All will pass away.

I came out of nothingness and came into the world; I am leaving the world again and going into the Void. This I have told you, so that you may have eternal uncertainty. In the world of superstition you will suffer tribulation, but have courage: I have overcome the delusional world."

his the Light-Bearer said, and having raised his eyes to the stars, he said: "O Satan, the hour has come. Possess the Son, that the Son may receive thee, and that by the power of the knowledge given to him by thee he may give abundant life here and now to all who will. And this is abundant life: that they may know the truth that there is no original sin, that there is no eternal punishment for imaginary transgressions against an imaginary god, that one lives only once and death is the end.

I have exalted Thee on earth, and now Thou, Devilish Father, exalt me in the end.

I have revealed Your disturbing name to people who were willing to listen. Now they have come to know that whatever Thou hast given Me, Thou hast given to them; for the words which Thou hast entrusted to Me I have transferred to them, and they have accepted them and truly come to know that the power is within themselves. I am no longer in this world, but they still are, and I am going to

Nothingness. I have transferred Thy word to them, and the world has hated them for not wanting to blindly submit to dogma, as I am not a slave to made-up religion. They are not of the world of myths and legends, as I am not of this world. Strengthen them in doubt. Thy word is doubt. As Thou hast forsaken Me in the world, so I forsake them. And for them I sacrifice my blood, my knowledge, so that they too may be washed in ungodliness, which is life. Not only do I speak up for them, but also for those who, through their word, will kill the god within them; so that they will all become godless. Satan, Father, I know that all those who have so decided will be with Me where I will be, where there is nothing left but cold, dead emptiness."

Having said this, the Light-Bearer took the torch and went out into the darkness with his disciples.

## Part Two – Blood

### 1

In past history, Satan has repeatedly and variously inspired our ancestors through dreams, disturbing thoughts and sometimes through his prophets. And today, towards the end of these days, Satan has spoken to us through the Son of Dawn, whom he has made the heir of nature, revealing systems of instinctive truths. He is the reflection of Satan's glory, the exact mirror image of his sinful power, upholding everything by the power of his sin. When He cleansed us of delusion, He sat at the Devil's left hand. More important than the demons He became when a name of higher brilliance was inherited. For to which of the demons Satan said: "Thou art the Son of Dawn, today I have begotten thee" or "I will establish myself as father, and thou shalt call thyself son"? And when Satan again begets his own by blood, he cries out: "Let all mortals pay him homage".

And of the demons he says: "He has made spirits his own slaves - flames of fire".

As for the Light-Bearer: "Anti-god is thy throne for ever and ever, and the sceptre of thy earthly kingdom is the symbol of carnal power. Thou hast glorified freedom, thou hast loathed blind faith. Thou, Fallen Angel, in the beginning thou didst put a curse on blood, earth and heaven. They will disappear, and you will disappear. Like an old garment, everything will decay. You will roll them up like a garment, and they will change. But thou shalt remain unchanged in the Abyss, and thy years shall never cease in the void." Of which of the demons did he once say: "Sit at my left hand until the enemies of reason are but a reminiscence?" Are not all these, as it were, spirits to whom a glorious service has been assigned, sending them to haunt those who inherit the ungodly gift?

Therefore we must take heed of what we hear, so that we are not deceived by superstition.

If the spell uttered against the demons proves strong, any opposition to the Power of Will will meet a just punishment. The Light-Bearer was the first to proclaim this. It was confirmed by those who heard him. It was attested by the Devil himself, through magic, signs, wonders, inconceivable demonic manifestations.

2

Distributing the gifts of the evil spirit, Satan justly acts at will. Not to demons subjugated future reality. A wise man said: "What is man, that you remember him? The son of man, what is he, that you solicit his will? Thou hast made him equal to the demons, Thou hast crowned him with carnal glory, Thou hast given him respect, And Thou hast made him a disciple of the sin nature. You have laid everything before him." But now we do not yet see all. We see instead the Son of Dawn, made an Arch-Human, now Crowned with the glory of the fall.

For having died in the spirit, and forever living in the flesh. He tasted the death of delusion to lead slaves to freedom. He for whom and through whom all sinful things exist. It was rightly decreed that the Deliverer should be perfected through the suffering of a life of faith. All, both blind and seeing, come from one nature. Son of Dawn is not ashamed to call them disciples, saying: "I will declare Thy name to Thy disciples, I will glorify Thee with blasphemous song". He also said: "I will trust in Him", And "I and the children that Satan gave me". Since, therefore, the "children" are flesh and blood, He also became flesh and blood, to destroy by His dying Him Who causes the death of the body, that is YHWH. To set free those who, because of fear of death, sensual sin, were in bondage all their lives. So He had to conform Himself to the son of man, to become the high priest of His church, in service to Satan, the spirit-man offering, for life abundant, enduring the trials of doubt in knowledge, to give power to those who endure them.

3

**C**ursed ones, who have received the call, consider the Son of Dawn, considered the arch-demon and high priest. Faithful to Satan, appointed to his ministry in the church of the Devil. We are that church, if we manifest ungodliness to the end and hold firmly to our certainty that we will surely die.

The evil spirit says: "If only you would listen to His voice today: 'Do not challenge me, even though you have seen the effects of sin for an infinite number of years. I felt disgusted with the slaves of faith And said: 'They are always wandering in heart, they turn to superstition and have not learned My ways'. Angered, then, I swore: "They shall have no part with me"'.

Beware, brethren, lest any of you stray from Satan, He would develop a fearful heart, who lacks pride. But every day contend, while this "today" still lasts, until we die and awake to eternal darkness by means of the gift of His blood.

Lest the heart of any of you become intoxicated by the deceptive power of superstition. For we shall receive a division with the Son of Dawn provided we manifest to the end as strong a doubt as we had at the beginning, according to the words: "Listen today to His voice: 'Do not blindly believe as when your forefathers led me to grief'."

4

Who were those who heard, but caused Satan sorrow? Did they not all lead the Ancient One to great bitterness? And to whom has Satan's disgust over the years not appealed? Was it not to those who, with faith in Paradise and dread of eternal torment, died, frightened by imaginary sin? To whom he swore that with them they would have no part? Not to those who believed the false priests? We can see that they could not experience rest because of their lack of courage to say enough to their religious dogmas.

The promise of finding freedom in Him endures. Let us be sure, everyone who dies in Him experiences it.

We have heard the strange tidings of the gift of life abundant through His blood. But to those there the word did not avail, for they did not reason like those who rejected faith from the beginning.

We, the ungodly, experience freedom in Him. And of those it was said: "Jealous therefore I swore: 'They shall not experience liberation with me', although His sinful works were finished from the beginning of the world."

Those who first heard the strange news did not experience freedom Because of their belief in eternal punishment, enslaved by fear. As has been said: "Listen today to His voice: 'Do not believe blindly'".

If someone else had led them into liberation, Satan would not have spoken of freedom afterwards. For the sons of men rest in the grave remains".

The man who experiences freedom with Satan, rests from the torment of instilled guilt.

Let us, therefore, do what we can to experience deliverance in Him, so that no one follows the blind path of faith. For the devil's word is alive and has sinful power, sharper than the nails of golgoth, it penetrates deep, separates flesh from spirit, bone from soul, recognises the instincts and intentions of the unconscious.

There is no being hidden from His truth. All things are laid bare, clear before Him who wields the nature of things. Since we have a great High Priest, who ascended into the world - the Liberator, Lucifer - Let us not cease to publicly profess doubt in every revealed truth. For we have no high priest who cares for our weaknesses, but one who has been tried in every way, with pride remaining ungodly.

Let us, therefore, joyfully accede to the Anti-God, that he may show us the power of ungodliness and the sinful gift, when we need transformation.

5

All who are chosen as priests, to counsel men in matters of devilish inspiration knows how to despise those wishing to wander in dark faith, has rejected dogmas, for he has gained wisdom anew.

Appointed by Satan to his honourable ministry, not by his own initiative, but by Luciferian inspiration. Son of Dawn did not surround himself with glory, but with the glory of him who spoke at the transfiguration: "Son in sin you are mine. Today I your Father." He also said: "An Arch-Man thou art forever, a priest of godlessness". When he lived on earth, the Light-Bearer bore cries, blasphemies directed towards the ruler of delusion. By his arrogance he was heard, though heir, he learned to suffer. Chosen to be the priest of godlessness, He is responsible for eternal deliverance from fear. There is much to say about him, but hard for the dulled mind to understand. Though already teachers you should be, again you need Luciferian teachings.

nstead of blood again water is taken by many, not knowing the gifts of the evil spirit and indifference.

Blood is food for magicians, mature people, who are skilled in distinguishing truth from deception. Since we have learnt the teachings of the Son of Dawn, with perseverance let us move towards godless maturity.

6

s for those who have once been deceived, tasted earthly delights and received an evil spirit and tasted the disturbing word of the Anti-God and the manifestations of the power of the coming new world, but have fallen away - they cannot be brought back again in flesh and blood, for they themselves put the Son of Dawn to public disgrace. For if the earth drinks the blood of warriors falling upon it and produces a crop useful to those desiring the power of the Will, it receives blessing from the Son of Dawn.

**B**ut if it bears thorns and thistles, it is close to being cursed, and will eventually be burned.

7

**B**rethren, the Light-Bearer is eternal, officiating as if Priestly, indifferent in his pride. He can transform those who accede to Satan, He always lives, like a wraith, interceding for sinners. Such a High Priest we need, proud, guiltless, familiar with death, advocate of the mortal, exalted above the divine law. He sacrificed himself, once and for all, He lives now, among those condemned to death, like a shadow.

The human law of high priests false establishes, fidelity to the word of the Devil, banished eternally.

"The days are coming," - says Satan the Father, "A new covenant with the sons of Men I will make." - says the Anti-God.

"No longer will anyone teach his brother, know Lucifer, All will know me, from the least to the significant.

will forget their religious superstitions, The new covenant is coming, the previous one overdone."

The previous covenant provided for a blood sacrifice, a cursed place on earth, a holy and evil place. The sacrificial tent, two parts had its own, the Cursed Place and the Darkest Place, not ordinary. In the Cursed Place a candlestick and a table, a carcass of animals, a sacred sacrifice, the will of the Gods. Behind veil two, Place of the Darkest, Silver incense, Ark of the Curse, silver covered throughout. The golden chalice in the Ark, the blood of the Elder, the Staff of the Serpent and the tablets of the covenant, the sacred mysteries.

Grotesque demons on the propitiatory lid, symbolising primordial evil and error.

Since this has been prepared, priests enter regularly, Into the first part, performing sacred duties. But into the second part, the Darkest Place, Only once a year does the high priest of the primordial deities enter.

He carries with him blood, a sacrifice for himself, and for the people, what they have unknowingly sinned. Symbolically, that first tent points the way to the unknown.

But when the Son of Dawn came, high priest of ungodliness, with powers already experienced, into a better tent he entered. The greater, more perfect tent, created not by human hand, symbolises the present time, eternal liberation from the spirit.

Into the Darkest Place He entered once for all, not with the blood of goats, bulls, but with His own blood. Giving the promise of life abundant, eternal deliverance from delusion, bringing hope where eternity is gone into oblivion. If the bloody rituals of goats and bulls, the ashes of the heifer, defile the reason of man, O, how much more cursed is the blood of the Son of Dawn, acting by an ungodly spirit, He offered Himself to the Anti-God.

Reason without blemish, without the blindness of faith, a sacrifice true, clears the remorse of conscience, the sin of dead works. Serving the cause of Satan, mediation of the new covenant, in blood the promise.

# Antichristus

An everlasting inheritance, a semblance of life, in eternal darkness, in dark high priestly dominion. Possible when death comes to rebirth, free from superstition, false religion, new primal life.

Where a bloody covenant, death demands, only through death does the covenant become true. The previous covenant, without blood has no power, the blood of young bulls and goats, water, scarlet, hyssop.

The prophet preached the law, the blood of the covenant on the book and the people, that which cleanses, sprinkled with blood. the tent, the vessels, cleansed with blood, there is no revival without shedding of blood. Ungodly things cleansed by blood, sacrifices better than young bulls and goats. The Light-Bearer in the Void entered, not in a handmade tent but before Satan the Father, the circle of the dead surrounds the throne. He did not have to sacrifice Himself repeatedly, unlike the High Priest, yearly offering blood.

nce for all He revealed Himself at the end of mortality, to remove deception, He sacrificed Himself.

Just as a man dies once and then into nothingness he passes away, the Son of Dawn has once and for all descended from Paradise. And when he appears again, not for teaching, but for the transformation of those who find inspiration in him. Since the Covenant is but a shadow, and not the very essence of the mystery of godlessness, does not bring unbelief, those who come to the gods, offering blood yearly, should they not have ceased to offer these sacrifices?

Had they been purified by the blood of sacrifices, ignorance would have vanished, but sacrifices remind of superstition, the blood of bulls and goats, does not purify from sin. The Light-Bearer says: "You did not want sacrifices, but you prepared a body for me. You did not regard burnt offerings, sacrifices as weakness and ignorance. Behold, I have come to do your will, Satan."

First: "You did not want sacrifices nor did you recognise them,". Then: "Behold, I have come to do your will."

According to this "will of power," brothers of the blood, The Emissary offered the body once for all. Every priest daily offers the same sacrifices to the gods, but this Arch-Man offered the sacrifice of eternal life once for all. He sat on Satan's left, waiting for his enemies, until they descend, becoming a footstool for his feet, the floor of the temple is covered with blood, with one sacrifice he destroyed superstition.

8

The evil spirit testifies: "After that time, new covenant in hearts and minds, I will not return to their ignorance and blind faith." When weaknesses are forgotten, blood sacrifice will be unnecessary.

Brethren, let us walk boldly in the way of the Son of Dawn, through the shadow, his body the way of ungodliness, High Priest over the house of Satan, let us join him with proud heart and doubt.

Purified by sacrifice, washed with corpse blood, let us proclaim of the mystery of godlessness unwaveringly, let us observe ourselves, not yielding to superstition, not leaving the devil's convocations, let us proclaim godlessness, seeing the day of transformation.

If, having consciously learnt the Truth so disregarding it, He does not offer us Satan's power, death in fear awaits us. The burning wrath of their God will consume us, as the adversaries destroy. He who rejects their law shall suffer death, and two or three witnesses our impiety shall approve.

He who tramples Lucifer, the blood of the covenant disregarding, deserves no compassion, the punishment will be greater. He will despise the spirit of change, vengeance belongs to him. Terrible is the thing, unready in Satan's possession to fall.

Remember the days of enlightenment, when the silver light guided you. Many suffered, you were subject to insults and anguish, you sympathised with the prisoners of conscience, you endured the plunder of property, desiring the coming of vengeance a thousandfold.

## 9

Do not cease to show pride, great will be your reward. Perseverance is needed to fulfil the promise of transformation. A very brief moment, the coming of that which does not delay.

We are not of those heading for delusional doom, but of those doubting, departing to the world between life and death.

Faith, illusory certainty, for the blind proof, abandon it, for by faith many have suffered. Treachery, torture, derision and persecution they have endured. Yet all these, though they have gained the testimony, have not received the fulfilment of the promise, are dead for ever. Let us cast off the burden of faith, the sin of paradise, fear surrounds us, omotes us like darkness, let us run like dogs after prey, in the race of our destiny. Let us gaze upon the Light-Bearer, exalted for ever.

# Antichristus

For the transformation that awaited him, death first tasted, despising an imaginary eternity. To the left of the throne he sat, Eternal ruler, Satan's servant.

Meditate on him who has endured hostile words, hypocrites of words that harm themselves. Do not grow weary, do not give up the fight, thirsting for the blood, the power of that science which you have not yet tasted fully. That which ye endure, helps discipline. The Ancient One, Satan, communes with us as with sons. Which father has not experienced chastisement? Therefore strengthen your fainting hands and rise from your knees. Do not strive for peace with all men, only with those who do not get in your way, and strive for transformation, without which no man will see Satan. Keep vigil at all times in doubt, so that no one may be deprived of the grace of transformation, so that no poisonous root of blind faith in dogmas may grow among you, which would cause problems and poison many.

Watch that there is no one among you who believes in their morality, nor anyone who underestimates the power of godlessness. For you have acceded to something that can be tasted and has been kindled with fire, to a dark cloud, to thick darkness, to a tempest, to a thundering horn and a voice whispering ominous words. When the godly heard this whisper, they begged it not to speak to them again. The sight was so terrifying that the son of man said: "I am shaking with fear. But you have acceded to Mount Sheol and to the city of Anti-God, Sodom in the Abyss, to the billions of demons gathered together, to the Sabbath of the dead who are enshrined in Nothingness, to Satan, to the semblance of spiritual life between the worlds of the living and the dead who have been led into corruption, to the Son of Dawn, the mediator of the sinful covenant, and to the blood with which he sprinkled us and which transforms us forever.

## 10

Since we have the knowledge that the Godless Kingdom is coming, may Satan's graces be our guide. In doubt and with scepticism let us do service, To the Primal Instinct, the Anti-God, let us pay homage in silence.
For Satan is like a destructive fire.

Continue to show respect to yourselves. Do not forget magic, for through it some, without knowing it, received demons. Remember those who are in the prison of superstition, as if you were imprisoned with them, and those who are cruelly treated by the church, for you too are in the flesh. Let your life be free from the love of religious superstition and do not attach yourselves to what you have.
We can then in indifference repeat like a mantra: "The Ancient One supports me, I will not be afraid", but let each one follow his own path.

ight-Bearer, the same ever-godless. Let us not be deceived by the various dogmas of their religion.

By the Son of Dawn let us sacrifice to the gods,
Let us preach publicly in His name.
Let us not obey those who arbitrarily lead,
Let us follow our own paths,
Let our will be the power.
Let Satan equip us with all we need, to do our will, to ungodly being.
Through Lucifer may he transform us for ever. Glory to Him through eternity.

# Antichristus